Eyar is a poet who has compiled this anthology of original poetry called *My Ups and Downs*. Eyar uses poetry to express the good and bad moments of his life. He has found a creative outlet through poetry, using it to discuss topics such as his mental health, the realisation of his Cerebral Palsy and his experiences as a transman.

Although all poems were written from 2015 to 2018, please note that some poems were written retrospectively. Please also note this collection of poetry only talks about events up until 2018, so be mindful that opinions expressed may have changed after 2018.

Eyar Berman-Roth

MY UPS AND DOWNS

AUSTIN MACAULEY PUBLISHERS™

LONDON • CAMBRIDGE • NEW YORK • SHARJAH

A CIP catalogue record for this title is available from the British Library.

ISBN 9781528935234 (Paperback)
ISBN 9781528968188 (ePub e-book)

www.austinmacauley.com

First Published (2019)
Austin Macauley Publishers Ltd
25 Canada Square
Canary Wharf
London
E14 5LQ

Firstly, I wish to thank my family, both blood and chosen, and everyone else who has supported me in both my poetry and my life in general. Your love and support mean more to me than I can ever say! You've all given me the strength to become the man I am today and the courage to put myself out there and publish this anthology! I love you all so much!

Secondly, I wish to thank my publisher, Austin Macauley, including everyone involved in the production and publication of this anthology. It means so much to me! I have wanted to publish this anthology for a long time, so thank you for making my dream a reality!

Thirdly, I wish to thank you, dear reader, for purchasing and reading this anthology. Words can't even begin to express how much that means to me, so thank you so much! I really hope you enjoy this anthology as much as I enjoyed creating it!

Table of Contents

Picture This

Picture this:
You've spent your whole life up 'till now in a daydream;
A haze, a fantasy—your own little utopia.
You knew nothing else.

Yet, in the back of your mind, right in the corner, resides a voice; a voice so small it's practically inaudible, yet present still.

One day, everything changes.

You're out in society as usual. Hang on... one stare... And another... And another. What's this? You've never noticed this before. Try to ignore it—trifling matter.

But you can't. The voice in your head starts to grow.
And grow,
And grow,
AND GROW!

By the time you're home,
The voice in your head is screaming.
You look in the mirror,
And you see it.
For the first time in your life,
You see it:
You're a cripple.

For the first time in your life, you realise what this means;
How you could never walk unaided
Like you always dreamed of.

How the term 'Cerebral Palsy' is significant for the very first time.

And all this time,
That voice hollers out:
"You should've listened to me! That's right, you're a cripple, you fool! You can't do anything! You're worthless, hopeless, a CRIPPLE!"

And what can you do?
Each word stabs like a knife.
But what can you do?
So you just agree with the voice,

And sob into the carpet.

Stick Girl

Stick girl, you okay?
Standing there with a piece of you missing;
What is it? A mouth.
Do you remember when you used to smile?

You reach out a hand. I touch it.
And it withers, crumbles away,
Making dark scribbles on the paper.

There's one line left; a remainder of your hand.
I pick it up. And bend and bend, and bend,
And bend and bend, and bend and bend
Stop!
Stop the pain!
There's nothing to gain here. No hope.

I place the line on your face,
Trace the cracks in the gravel,
Trace the tears on your cheek.
When were you last happy?
When was it?

Step back. Look hard. It's me.

In the Wind

It's you. You're in the wind,
In my heart, everywhere.
Kiss me, touch me, hold me tight.

Who you are, I know not,
Nor when we will meet.
But I feel you, even though we're strangers;
You're in the wind.

We both have flaws, you and I,
But together, we are one;
We'll balance each other out,
And love each other for who we are;
Love each other through the good and the bad,
The wonderful and the ugly,
You'll see.

But right now, I just want you to know this:
Even now I am utterly, hopelessly, madly,
Truly, unconditionally, irretrievably in love with you,
I just don't recognise you yet.

So let the wind bring us together,
Let fate take its course,
There's no need to rush.
I know we'll find each other,
I can't wait to call you mine.
We'll release a tide of invisible sparks,
As the wind circles serenely round us.

Movement

Trapped.
Not entirely, yet enough still.

To move is an asset society takes for granted.
After all, movement is one of the foundations of life, of expression: with movement, you could paint Starry Night or pilot a NASA space shuttle; the possibilities are so infinite that movement should be considered as magnificent as the human brain and speech!

So, answer me this question:
What happens to those of us who are deprived of the ability to control movement either partly or entirely? What do we do when we feel short-circuited and trapped in a biological machine that was intended to benefit us?

I'll tell you what we do. We find the song of life and we dance.
Life is precious, so make the most of it, no matter what. Your dance is your own! Be the person you want to be!
We may be restricted externally, but inside, we're always dancing!
And I for one,
Will never stop.

Have You?

Have you ever had the feeling
That you want to express yourself,
But don't know how?

Have you ever felt like something deep inside you
Is waiting,
Just waiting,
To break free?

Have you ever felt like
You're made up of two people: the internal person is the one
That does everything you wish you
Could do,

While the external person
Keeps jerking you back
Into reality;
A move that's painful every time.

Tell me, have you ever
Doubted your capabilities,
Or wanted to scream,
Cry,
Run,
Die?

Have you ever
Experienced the pain
Of death? Of having someone you love
Whipped off this earth, even if they're far too young?
Or did you see your entire world

Come crashing down, reduced to ashes
In front of your very eyes? Everything you ever knew,
Suddenly burnt and broken.

But, have you ever
Woken up in the morning,
And known that tomorrow will come,
And everything will be okay again?
That you're stronger than you think?
That you'll breathe again?
That there is hope?

Well, have you?

Mirror

I raise my left hand.
You raise your right.
Standing there, looking at me.

The same face as my own.
Same eyes.
Mouth.
Hair.

Yet, we are different people;
While I'm confident and optimistic,
You're depressed and fretful.

Your presence is rare,
But you ignite in me such an acute pain,
That you consume me entirely;
Withering away my confidence,
Until mere rubble is left.

And here you are again.
I feel you. Your presence is undeniable,
Just as it was when I was chronically depressed.
Why do you grieve so?
Is it life?
Has it all just become too much to handle?
I'm part of you.
You're part of me.
Bound forever.

I know this is a dip in mood;
I know you sometimes have doubts,
And now you're cold;
But come. Take my hand.
Don't be afraid.
Together, we can,

Fix me.

Highlighter

10:15 am.
Staring at work, highlighter in hand.
Silence.

I stare at the orange line that seems to go A.W.O.L from the words destined to be highlighted. Okay, you can do this, Eyar! You can do this! Try again: start highlighting. Zigzag, Zigzag. The line still disobeys my hand's command, but it's better now; I can live with that. I drop the highlighter. Crash! Piercing through the silence. Great! Gently pick it up—hands fail to grasp. Come on! Grab it! Just grab the highlighter—got it! Breathe. Calm down. Good. Now, just pass the highlighter to your right hand so I can adjust it—that's it! Well done! My right hand quivers. Quick! Left hand, grab it! Phew! I am panting now. Face glistening with perspiration, sweat patches on my shirt. Wow! Why did that cause such an exertion? It's only a highlighter. I could've asked for help, I know I could. But I desire the satisfaction of independence more than I can even comprehend.

Now, where was I?

Been There, Done That

My sisters call me old; and I mean around the age of 90. This isn't helped by the fact that my soul's considered to be 'ancient' on an online personality quiz. You should know, I will quite literally pour my heart out to you every single time we converse in conversation. But, even if I don't always reveal everything, I will always reveal some aspect of the truth. Should life decide to hurl spears in my direction, I will combat them like Jackie Chan; although my high kicks might be a little off! And if, by chance, one of the spears enters my heart, I will stagger—not fall, stagger, with pride to a corner, and tenderly lick my wounds. I shall return with my scars more than visible, starting over and over until I have the strength and tenacity in my soul to say: "Been there, done that." No matter how much you've "been there" or "done that", nothing gets easier; you just get better at handling it.

The entire surface of the back of my hands is punctuated with needle marks that can be regarded as significant as a birthmark; something that shouldn't be worth evaluation. Yet, because it is so explicitly placed, it becomes a special part of you and only you. Still, every time I have a blood test, the sight of the needle makes me a little nervous for the first two seconds. And don't even get me started on operations! You know the saying "I've got the T-shirt"? Well, I have an entire outfit: a white, pristine outfit that if it were real, would probably smell of the alcohol used in hospitals.

People ask me how I'm able to ricochet from adversity. I grin and say: "It's part of the fun." Admittedly, sometimes it isn't fun, but it makes me stronger; being thrown into cold water gives me thicker skin to swim with.

So, you may look into my eyes and see that they bare the look of scars way before my time. But these old eyes just mean I can say: "been there, done that!"

Crush

I know this is cliché, but there's this guy—I know, not a great start, we all know where this goes—but hear me out. I'm now in my first year of Sixth Form, and there's this guy who, I'm sure you've already guessed it, I'm very much attracted to. Isn't that great? I think so. But then again, I'm the one with these emotions, so I guess that makes me biased. Crushes are bizarre: one moment you're perfectly fine and the next you fix your eyes on someone, and that's when the emotions start! Others are gradual. In this case, we're dealing with the former. I've tried to get to know him. This is going okay; much better than my high school crush: he was the sole reason I went red at school—and I mean heart palpitations, shy, on the verge of fainting sort of crush—like the ones you see in movies. That lasted three years! Anyway, we're getting off topic: my current crush, who I cannot mention the name of, in case he reads this, seems lovely. We've had some nice conversations and I'm starting to be attracted to his personality. If this continues, I may be susceptible to falling in love with him.

Woah, woah, woah, hang on! Slow your horses! What did you just say? Did you just say what I think you just said? You barely know him! My head talks sense. Thank you, head. But you don't need to worry just yet. I never said I was falling for him, simply that I might do in the future if I get to know him better. My attraction is just as violent as in high school—I can just handle it better. Thank god! I'm not looking to be with him, if that's what you think. I just want to get to know him. And if anything comes of it, great!

Man, crushes are weird!

The Worst Thing He Ever Did

A colleague. Knew each other from
Nursery.
When sucking my dummy was a scheduled routine during
nap-time,
I'd see him sneak out of bed.

Year 1: He decided to propose to me. That innocent time when
all the adults think it's adorable to perform such an act; it
probably is, but I declined on the bases that "I wanted to find
my own husband", as I had apparently put it. He left it at that.

He then decided to kiss me in our school swimming pool; the
result of seeing my father giving me a goodbye kiss. I honestly
don't remember what it felt like, so I don't count it as my first
kiss.

Jump to Year 3: I'd just gotten my spelling results back, when
out of nowhere, his hand meets my right eye. The TA gives
me a cold tissue; he goes to the principal's office. He comes
back, he apologises. I forgive him.

Year 4: He starts fighting with teachers: hitting and biting,
pinching and scratching. No number of timeouts convinced
me he wouldn't hurt me again.

Year 5: Our relationship confused me: I considered him a
friend even though dad said it's okay not to like some people.
I don't like not liking people. And besides, he was helpful—
sometimes.

Year 6: I make the mistake of telling my best friend that I had a small crush on him whilst we all were having lunch. He was fine with it, but my colleague teased me.

Year 6: Afternoon gardening. I find myself seated next to my colleague watching the TAs pick strawberries. His hand slides across my lap and touches my privates.

Year 6: In all the years I've known him, he's never done anything like this.
Year 6: I tell him to stop.
Year 6: He continues.
Year 6: I tell him to stop.
Year 6: He continues.
Year 6: I threaten to tell somebody if he doesn't stop. He stops.
Year 6: I try to forget about it.
Year 6: I can't.
Year 6: Something about it doesn't feel right. I tell my father.
Year 6: My father phones the school.
Year 6: I tell my teacher what happened.
Year 6: My colleague is separated from me.
Year 6: This goes on for some time.
Year 6: My colleague apologises. I forgive him.
When you're 11, you have no concept of what any of this means. Now that I do, I understand why I suffered rape nightmares for a fortnight after the incident; although it's not rape, it's still indecent assault, and that fact terrifies me more now than it did back then.
Despite this, I still forgive him. It's taken years, but I've managed to truly forgive him; giving forgiveness is part of what I do to live life to the full.

But that incident will always be,
The worst thing he ever did.

Eyes

I know this woman,
Who is very special to me.
We are very close,
and have a lot in common.

Her dominant emotion is the sort
Which only few possess;
Wild, untamed enthusiasm,
That lights me up in an instant.

Yet, on the very rare occasion,
She smiles as usual but,
There's a subtle pain
In her eyes.

On the even rarer occasion,
The pain moves to her countenance,
But mostly
Resides in her eyes;
Desperate not to be seen.

But I see it.
In those vibrant, wonderful eyes,
I see it.

I know not the pain she suffers;
I am too naive.
Her honesty is her best virtue.
So when I gaze into those eyes,
And pain haunts them,
My grief is of the acutest kind.

Why must such a woman,
Whose disposition is of the sweetest kind,
Suffer so?

She is my father's cousin.
But had she not been relation,
My affection would still be boundless.

And I wish her to know,
Though she may not believe me,
That my love and admiration for her
Is infinite.
We both know this life isn't easy,
But she's come through so much;
I may not know her pain,
But I know she's so strong!

I wish she could see herself
Through my eyes:
Strong yet fragile,
And an all-round wonderful person!
I love her so much!

I thank her
For confiding in me,
Even when it hurts,
And her pain threatens
To reduce us both
To tears.

She does not know what she means to me.
She cannot know;
It is too deep,
Too profound
To be described,
As is the case with everyone I love.

When I look into her eyes,
I know just how lucky I am
To have her,
In my life.

Grass (After "What Is the Grass?" by Mark Doty)

What's the word I'm looking for? Grass. Grass? No, that can't be right. Find an alternative: thorns, blades, knifes, grass. No! How many times have we been through this? Forget about grass! Don't forget, you want this to be analysed by thousands of students one day; want them to dissect every fraction of each word until the only debris left are the particles that make up the word itself. And yet, you are once again compelled to use the word, that vile word 'grass'! May I remind you that this is the fifth time you've attempted to complete this novel; always obviated by the incapacity to be fully comprehended! No one can understand the depths of me: the turmoil that pulsates through my veins and my every being! Especially, not some idle student, who is more than content to just read the word and conclude, with absolute certainty, that they know what was unfolding in the black cavern of the author's mind. Mine does not rest; it never will. But I must write 'grass', and hope someone will recognise my anguish.

The Stage (Inspired by Robert Browning's Dramatic Monologues)

I'm comfortable here. I really am. I've been on this stage, playing this role for so long, I've mastered it; the perfect actor. It's me, my stage, and anybody who cares enough to watch. I'm comfortable here. I really am. I'm an expert at this by now! After all, it's been so long since I did anything else— get a hold of yourself! Sorry, what I meant to say was I love this job—I do! There's really nothing better! I mean, giving people what they want to see isn't bad, right? Except… I don't know how much longer I can keep this up—no! Pull yourself together! You're an actor, for God's sake! Everything's fine, stay in role! Stay in role, stay in role, stay in role! No, no, no! Don't break, don't break, don't break! No one can handle it! You can't handle it! Just keep acting! You're comfortable here, remember? You said it yourself, so believe it! Don't break, never break!

There's a reason I avoid eye contact;
People might see the truth.

Forgiveness

What do you do,
When you receive that fatal knock
On the door?

What do you say,
When you're standing at
The funeral of a loved one?

There is nothing.
Nothing we can say,
Or do. Nothing to stop
The gaping hole,
That engulfs you entirely.

So, we resort to asking for forgiveness:
Forgiveness for not realising that the last conversation can be
as simple as
"Hi".
Forgiveness for not trying to make the final embrace
Last forever.
Forgiveness for not foreseeing that the car would turn
Over,
And over,
And over,
And over.
That's all it took.

I am no different:
So, Stacey,
You didn't die in a car accident, but,
Forgive me.

Forgive me for not knowing that Muscular Dystrophy
Had rendered you ill, powerless.
Forgive me for not knowing you were hospitalised;
No one told us.

Forgive me for not saying goodbye;
For making our last conversation
"Hi": a fleeting moment in the corridor.
Forgive me for crying; I know you'd kick my butt, but
I didn't know what else to do;
The pain was too acute.

The pain never truly vanishes: it subsides with acceptance,
but never vanishes.
I love you, Stacey. You were my best friend,
And you left this world too young—you were only twelve.
I don't know if you knew this was coming, but,
Thanks for your forgiveness over everything
That happened after your death.
I know you're well.
Maybe I'll see you again someday.

Used to Be Mine

It's funny how life tends to leave its stain on people;
That bloody mark of vengeance of depression somehow
echoes: "You're no match for me! I'm stronger than you, and
you know it!"

The depression you caused broke me; the fragments of my
inner being lay scattered on the sea-coloured carpet where I
drowned and choked on my tears. It watched me, and mocked
my agony, knowing that if I had the capability, I would've
happily entered the portal where I could be free from your
chains that used to diminish me.

Cerebral Palsy,
You saved my life.
Ironic as that may seem,
Had your chains been a fraction weaker;
Had I been able to climb to the window,
Had I been able to secretly purchase a pistol,
I would not be here.

So no, I don't hate you. In fact, I thank you for saving my life.
I have recovered the fragments of myself slowly, slowly and
ever so painfully. Now, a plaster the size of Russia holds me
together. I will not break over my disability again. But the
wound bleeds now and again. I'm not who I used to be:

Do you remember
The pure, unadulterated
Joy that danced on the face
Of a girl that looked like me?

That kind of joy no longer exists; in its place, a joy tainted with a mountain of acceptance. And the fire that blazed fiercely in her eyes whenever she did anything, now exists as a black spark.

I'm not the same.

I would ask you to let me see the girl I once knew again. But you won't do that, will you? You can't. The hands on the clock only turn one way, don't they?

I would give anything
To spend time with the girl
That used to be mine.
I miss the unadulterated joy she had.
But she's gone. I lost her. I lost the person I was without warning. And that's why I am nostalgic; so I can see her again for as long as I remember the moment.

So, you can mock the blood
I've bled these last few days,
As I remember the happiness of a time
When I was ignorant to your existence.
You can do this, but you know just as well as I do that my heart will heal before I return to school. I've a lump in my throat that won't subside at the moment, but I know it will eventually.
I'll be okay.

I just want to say something
To the girl who used to be mine:
Though you've left me, I stand here and state that though I'm not the same without you, I understand my disability now; I understand it, and there's nothing wrong with it. Though my future happiness will not be in the same nature as your blissful ignorance, I'm trying to find a new type of happiness. I'm stronger for having this disability, and I believe a better type of happiness will be mine one day.
I just wanted to tell you I'm okay.

Come on, Come Out

There you are:
I've been looking for you forever.
Come on,
Come out.

You've stayed hidden for too long;
The quiet soul in a loud voice.
Come on,
Come out.

I can't lie, I'm just
As vulnerable as you,
Right now.
Nervous about what impression
This will have.

But everything will be okay.
One day, the distinction between us will blur,
And we will be one.

You're smiling now,
And so am I;
The childhood fantasy excites you,
Does it not? Turned out to be real;
Just as your 5-year-old self wanted it to be,
But never thought possible.

We must be patient;
Both you and I.
But, it'll be worth it
When you replace me.

So come on,
Come out;
Tell your parents.
There's nothing to fear.

The only difference
People will ever see,
Is I will be,
My parents' son.

Words

Hate is a strong word,
I know.
And I know that you should never hate anything,
But it's hard.
Because the truth is,
The unbearable truth is,
I detest the word 'lady' and all its other lexemes
When addressed to me:
When my mother called me 'girl' the other day,
It sent daggers to my heart.
And the fact that one of my recent awards is a 'female' award,
Is enough to make me want to tear the certificate to shreds.

I know I used to accept these words,
But that was before I understood my identity as male.
Now that I do, I can't stand being referred to as female, or
with female lexemes anymore;
It's not who I am.

But it's difficult for everyone. I understand.
I can't expect anybody to call me otherwise:
I don't appear masculine; in any way.
And I'm still closeted to most of society,
Who knows when I'll be able to come out publicly?
But oh, how I hate these sickening words
That mock my existence.

4,183 Miles

4,183 miles.
That's the distance between you and me. If I'm honest, it feels greater.

Fun fact: the first YouTube video I saw from you was the one about
Coming out to your mum. I felt your pain acutely. And then,
When you made that video about the prospect of not pursuing happiness in this lifetime, I reached out to you. Told you my pain; the forbidden tears sleeping at the back of your eyes mirroring my own.

There are days when it hurts to breathe; to be alive with hearts as tumultuous as ours. If only the distance between facade and authenticity was 4,183 miles. If only the distance between fear and prosperity was 4,183 miles. If only transitioning was as simple as catching the next flight to Nashville to see you.

4,183 miles.
That's the distance between me and you. If I'm honest, it feels greater. But sometimes I close my eyes, and you are here by my side. And I am by yours.
And I promise, the distance will never break the unspoken connection we have. You give me hope that I can be the man I'm meant to be. I promise to do the same for you, no matter what!

I know you can reach the stars. I put my faith in you like you put your faith in me! We can do this together! Let's both make this life,
Worth living.

Don't Ask Me to Tell
You I Don't Love You

Don't ask me to tell you I don't love you.
Spare me that pain.
Please. Wait. Don't
Ask me to tell you I don't love you.

We bare the same first name;
Yet, you are a woman,
And I'm a man: a man who must stand on his own two feet
now,
Not yours.
But that doesn't mean I don't love you.

I love you. Always have. Always will.
But this can't work anymore:
You know as well as I do
That we—I have been this way since puberty.
And that's not going to change;
You know that now.

Don't ask me to tell you I don't love you,
You know it's not true.
If I could stand in front of you,
I would caress your tear-stained cheeks,
Look into your eyes, let you know that I love you.
Because I love you.

And it's because I love you, that I must do this;
I have to let you go.
I have to let you go so that I can be me.

I don't hate you,
But it's for the best.
You've always wanted us—me to be happy.
So I have to let you go.

But just before you go,
You should know,
That I love you.

How Does It Feel?

You ask me how it feels,
To be a boy.
The familiar lump makes itself at home in my throat. I'm a little
Thrown by the question.

For how does it feel to be a boy when the mirror has your reflection wrong?
I do not have the language to answer that question. All I have is—

Flashback: I'm in year 10; by this point, I'm used to telling people I don't feel I'm feminine, and letting them contradict it, not knowing how to express how I feel—how I've felt since I was twelve.

Flashback: year 11: mum says: "I want you to be feminine for prom." Don't say anything. Bite your tongue. You want to say you don't feel feminine; that you feel like a boy, but bite your tongue. Can't say anything; mum would flip, and you wouldn't want to disappoint anyone—let's face it, mum would be the most likely person to be disappointed, and you don't have a good relationship with her. Besides, mum, of all people, wouldn't understand; she'd think you're crazy, or misinterpreting. And you also think you're crazy at this point! Keep supressing, keep supressing, keep supressing.
Flashback: You're in a dress looking in the mirror as mum air-brushes your face with makeup. Don't dare contradict her. Mother knows best. But you hate it! The dress is bad enough, but the make-up is worse! You're very uncomfortable and want to take it all off, but at least, mum's happy. You didn't

have the money for a tux, anyway. Go to prom. Have a great time. Always acknowledge the awkwardness you feel when not doing anything. Acknowledge how much you wanted the tux. Acknowledge this would've been so much more comfortable, and much less awkward, with the tux. But sigh and leave it at that.

Come out. For God's sake, just do it. Mum's reaction was just as predicted, dad was supportive after two weeks, and your sisters were confused. Okay, let's face it, the whole family was confused, but it'll take time to adjust. Get miss-gendered all the time; everywhere. Remember to be thankful for any complement whenever around anybody. Start using male pronouns with dad when speaking Hebrew and English—your sisters aren't ready to do that yet, and mum's still in denial. Isolate yourself during gender dysphoria. Cry, just cry. Take therapy. Know you're doing the right thing. It gets better, just be yourself.

How does it feel to be a boy?
It feels... right.

Tennis Match

I'm a human tennis match;
Swinging to-and-fro between being depressed and neutral.
Luv-fifteen to depression.

Being 'neutral' is the closest I can get to happiness:
A state where I can rationalise my emotions without being
truly happy,
To prevent myself from crumbling. 'Neutral' is a state where
I'm okay enough to cope. It's been like this for almost a year
now.

My life is a tennis match.
On the days that 'neutral' has the upper hand,
I'm able to rationalise the situation: "Just five more months
until the gender clinic, you're going to be okay." Fifteen all.

My gender dysphoria is a beast;
Overwhelms me completely.
And with its strength, my emotions and depression become
intractable.
I try to control them,
But depression is too strong an opponent;
Uses my gender dysphoria as a catalyst to attack me further,
Turns my emotions against me,
Leaving me to try and salvage my shattered hope;
But this swinging to-and-fro,
This back and forth,
Is killing me.
Every time 'neutral' swings,
Depression swings harder. Suddenly, it's 30-40 to depression.
My life is a tennis match.

And I am a spectator. A spectator who feels everything.
Every "you're going to be okay", every mis-gendered pronoun, every "even though your heart is breaking, it will be worth it! Hang in there!"

Match point.

For Mack

June 2016.
That's when we first met.
I, an angsty teen whose discovery of identity
Felt like learning how to walk again.

You, an equally angsty man,
Whose position as a closeted female-to-male
I knew all too well.

Yet, when you sent me an email with the words "Hey, this is
Mack from YouTube",
A ray of sunshine broke through the clouds;
I had found you.

Mack, perhaps I should explain:
You see, I just could not contain
My emotions. Which is why, at that time,
I was lucky to have met you—more than lucky.
Life is a journey.
But I wouldn't have gotten through the past year without these
things: you, my family, my school counsellor and everyone
else who has supported me.

Life is a journey.
And as I got to know you,
With your smile and joy,
I came to regard you as one of the best friends
I've ever had.

You're truly something special, Mack;
A beacon of light in my life.

You make me feel that I can make it through the darkness,
To a new dawn.

Fast forward to the present—February 2017.
You're out of the closet and starting Testosterone,
And I am right behind you;
Freedom will be mine soon enough.
I don't know when all of this will happen to me,
But I know you'll be right beside me.
Yesterday is history, tomorrow is a mystery, and today I have
you.

You're one of the best things that's ever happened to me.
You inspire me, Mack;
Your friendship inspires me to be the best I can be,
That we can both be the men we want to be,
Despite everything we've been through.
Despite all the pain,
We're making it through the rain,
And the sun shall shine again!

You make me a better man.
And I'm so happy and proud to see you become the man you
want to be.
I hope I help you as much as you help me.
Know that I've always got your back,
And someday we will both be free.

In the Waiting Room
of the Gynaecologist

In the waiting room of the gynaecologist,
There are purple seats.
Purple is a colour on the LGBTQ+ flag.

I look over at the women on these seats,
And wonder if they will be able to catch my heart
As it bursts through my chest; I do not know if I have
The strength to hold it.

In the waiting room of the gynaecologist,
All is calm. Yet, my insides tremble like an earthquake;
My house is crumbling, and I'm the only person who can
rebuild it again.

In the waiting room of the gynaecologist,
I sit: a man who can fool the world, but not himself.
A man who repeats the mantra:
*"It's okay, you're a man, you're a man, you're a man, it's
going to be okay"*,
Just to try and keep in control of a situation
That he has no control over.

Just because I'm here, does not mean I'm a woman;
Nothing could ever make me one.
I'm cold from my own sweat.
It's my first time here,
And the anxiety of having the area I can't even think about,
inspected, is too much to bear from a GP,
Let alone the gynaecologist.

I look over at my father.
He sits in the chair nearest to me, reading some sort of
magazine.
I want to hug him;
Want to sob in his arms, as he wraps me up in a bear hug,
But I don't. I know he knows how hard this is for me. I know
I could ask him,
But I don't. This gender dysphoria is my battle alone,
Like I said, I'm the only one who can rebuild this home,
So I stay silent.

My name is called. It's my turn.
Here goes—everything.

Mayday

Mayday!
Mayday!
Mayday!

They say you're the pilot of your life.
What happens when you lose control?
What then?

Mayday, mayday, mayday! Eyar, do you read?
My body, harbour of my soul,
Feels too tight;
I can't breathe,
Can't breathe at all.

I tried retracting within myself
To make this body feel like home,
But my demons lurk in the shadows;
Stab a glass shard into my heart
And watch the bleeding.
Leaving a desolate voice crying:
Mayday, mayday, mayday! Eyar, do you read?

My gender is a delicate rose;
I know it has the power to bloom if given half the chance,
But right now, all it's doing,
Is hurting me; thorns in my side make everything a trigger
warning,
And my mind screams:
Mayday, mayday, mayday! Eyar, do you read?

It's so hard to fight gender dysphoria,

When you have to constantly attend the gynaecologist's appointments;
A constant reminder that
This body is mine, but I do not own it.
Despite my best efforts, my dysphoria, anxiety and depression are too strong,
And I feel so small.

Mayday! Mayday! Mayday!
I'm falling apart. I'm crashing down.
I can smell the smoke
From my own malfunction.
I am not the pilot right now.
The external pressures are too great,
I can't cope.

I protect my family from this,
Build walls around myself,
So they don't get hurt when I self-destruct,
And it will stay this way.
For if they knew how bad it gets,
If they knew the darkest depths of me,
It'd be as if I were a stranger to them;

They wouldn't recognise me.
I've battled fluctuating gender dysphoria, depression and anxiety for so long;
Danced this four-way tango with them too many times.
And I'm tired. Of everything.

At the site of the plane crash,
Under the debris and rubble,
A radio, torn from its socket upon impact,
Crackles. If you listen closely,
You may hear a faint, fragile voice:
"I'm still here. Eyar, do you read?"

Manhood

Sometimes I watch him while I listen.
At the front of the class, his face in serene contemplation, a closed pen pressed lightly to his chin, his gentle eyes resting on whoever's speaking
As we fire philosophical theories, questions, answers that ricochet off the walls of the room; our own Pandora's box.

Sometimes I watch him while I listen.
He's my only male teacher this year. I watch his stubble crawl across his chin, catch the sight of his Adam's apple as he speaks.
He first taught me about Freud's theory of the human psyche, as evidence against some philosophical debate.
I found the concept of the id most interesting,
Considering it's part of the unconscious mind, filled with repressed desires,
Considering I now know how much of my desired manhood was unconsciously repressed during the wrong puberty.

On Wednesday, I told him my secret.
He now knows how the acne around my chin is my way of joining up the dots.
He knows how my brain sends imaginary testosterone signals into my bloodstream, at least for now.

After our meeting, he said: *"Let me know if I can give you any men's advice."* I thanked him.
He understood.

Letter to My Broken Self

Hi, Eyar,

I won't use the term 'dear'; I know you don't think you're worth that title, but let me assure you, you are very, very dear to me. I know you've a hard time believing anything right now, but it gets better. I know the question on your lips is 'when?' The phrase that scalds your tongue is "It will never get better", but it does. This is no easier for me to say than it is for you to believe it. Eyar, how can I ever forget the dark void that occupies your mind day in, day out? You never saw darkness until now. And I know how you wish you didn't feel like an outsider; how you would give anything to fit in, or be any other place but here—did you think you could hide that from me? Believe it or not, one day, you'll thank your disability for saving your life; it will be worth living.

I know you're only 10, but I must warn you, you'll lie to yourself for 4 years from the age of 12 without knowing it; don't ask me what it is about—you wouldn't believe me. It will take you many years to understand it, to feel it, but when you do, I promise everything will make sense: you'll understand why you lied—so don't be too hard on yourself. Guess what? By the time you come to understand everything I've mentioned in the latter part of this letter, you'll have become me. I already know that the road I'm travelling on is, and will be, much harder than anything you're experiencing now. I'd be lying if I said I haven't had depression again. I'd be lying if I said I haven't been suicidal again. I'd be lying if I said I'm not terrified; and I don't want to lie to you anymore. The fact I'm writing this letter to you means you're stronger than you think! So, I know this is a lot to ask, but I need you to get better. I need you to get better so that I have the strength to continue my journey. I know you can do it!

Go back to crying; I won't stop you.
But remember, I'll come for you one day.
I'm proud of you, Eyar.
Love,
Your future self.

In My Head

In my head,
There's a mountain
I climb every day.
I'm the only one who climbs it;
With nothing but hands for tools.

In my head,
The weather's more unpredictable than in England;
It changes spontaneously.
The world could not survive
The climate in my head.

In my head,
It's raining again today;
I've grown used to it,
It now rains most days.
There's a storm in my head again today,
But I must keep holding on.

In my head,
It's hard to climb
When it rains.
I always lose my footing.
Every. Single. Time.

I must keep climbing;
There is no other option.
I will climb this mountain
Until the day I die; it is the mountain of my life;
We all have our own life mountain to climb.
I have very little control of this mountain;

Or at least it feels this way.
More often than not,
The rain in my head inflicts more agony than
My physical pain ever could;
I can't climb the mountain with the rain like this.
There's such a storm in my head,
It's code red weather, whether warning.

So I curl up inside myself.
If I can make it through tonight,
I may have the strength to climb again,
Tomorrow.

Secret Confession

I pour my heart into these poems, so I might as well say this:
I really like you. And I mean <u>REALLY </u>like you.
Great! Now that my confession is at least written on paper,
I can proceed.

I apologise for my frankness;
You know I'm always honest.
And that means I need to be honest with myself,
But accept the fact that you may not feel the same;
That's why it has slept under my tongue for so long.

But sometimes, I wonder what it would feel like
To have your lips against mine, hold your hand, be with you.
'Cause damn, you make me want to be your boyfriend so
badly!

I have to be realistic, though.
The fact is you're my best friend,
Which is why this is problematic:
I can't risk things being awkward between us
Just because my heart's set in motion by the thought
Of your smile.
Your friendship is too important to me;
I never want to do anything to jeopardise what we have,
'Cause I've never had anything like it. I've never had a
friendship like the one I have with you.

So, the crush has to go.
I must get over you.
And though that's a painful realisation,
It's for the best.

You already mean so much to me. You know that.
And you should also know that this crush, as intense as it may
be, is not mistaken for love. Trust me, if I were in love with
you, it'd be a completely different story!

The irony is,
You will read this poem, you will hear my confession, all the
while oblivious that you are the subject.
But at least you'll enjoy the poem.

I must get over you.
It's going to be a struggle;
You're a tough one to get over.
But you're completely worth it.
And I'm honoured to be your friend.

Dear Friend

Dear friend,
We've always been honest with each other.
So I should tell you,
I'm in love with you.
You can't imagine how good
That feels to say out loud.

Dear friend,
I took my time with this;
Needed to be sure.
You are, after all, my best friend,
And I know this will make you blush.

Dear friend,
I promise, I never intended to fall for you;
Tried to get over the crush.
But maybe the reason I couldn't,
Was because I was falling for you.

Dear friend,
You know about the crush;
I told you myself.
This will surprise you,
But I've spent the last few days
Trying to deal with these emotions,
"For I can't help falling in love with you."
And I know that was cliché,
But you love Elvis!

Dear friend,
You are my first love.

Which gives you more reason to doubt me (as I had doubted myself),
But I've never felt like this before;
It's a peculiar warm-fuzzy feeling,
Much greater than anything I've felt before;
A burning,
Deep in my gut and heart.
And I've told you I believe we know
Love when we feel it.

Dear friend,
I used to believe,
Even without any experience,
That my heart loved whoever I was meant to spend my life with, without knowing who they are yet;
I even wrote a poem about it.
I don't know if I believe that anymore,
But I know I'm in love with you. I love you.

Dear friend,
I know you don't have romantic feelings for me.
And that's a realisation that hurts so badly;
There's a hole left to fill in my heart,
But I know you'll give it back gently.

Dear friend,
Do not worry about me.
This poem has no agenda
Other than to vent;
You know how much I like to do that.
This is the only way I know how,
And telling you my feelings will help me move on.

My dear friend,
I'm already making peace
With this unrequited love.
Your friendship is a comfort to me;
For it's better to have you in my life as a friend,

Than not at all.
And with this knowledge,
My pain is eased.
That's why I can find the strength
To finally let you go, and be *"easy like Sunday morning"*.
You don't have to say anything:
I won't say anymore after this poem,
I promise.

My dear friend,
I know you well. It's a privilege to call you a friend.
Thanks for being there,
Through thick and thin.
I hope we continue to have great fun as we always have done,
I will love you platonically, for all that you are.
You'll be one of the first to know about my future love interests and relationships!
Oh, and by the way, I'm still buying you that tux one day!

A Response to the Statement: "You Work Too Hard"

A response to the statement: "you work too hard":

This is probably true. I'm a self-identified workaholic, after all.
Don't be surprised if you see me with scarily veiny eyes,
Like cartoon characters who can't get enough sleep.

My studies and I have a complicated relationship:
It knows that most days,
I wish I didn't have to commit myself to yet more work.
But it also knows,
That it is my saviour.

It is the only thing I have full control over.

Life is a whirlwind. A tornado. A rushing current that flows through our very being,
Lifting us up,
Crashing us down.
And sometimes, I can't keep up.

When the anxiety of having to validate
My own gender is too much weight on these shoulders;
When it feels as if this world will swallow me whole,
Before spitting me onto a concrete wall,
My studies are always there; a secure base in all this madness.

I believe in the existence of free will, albeit limited.
And I choose this. Even if I don't want to study,

To be honest, most of the time I don't want to study.
But since I'm still in education,
I choose to work to the best of my ability,
To prove that I, am worth something.

It's so easy for me to feel worthless,
To allow the gender dysphoria, anxiety and depression to hijack me;
And if I'm honest, they still do.
That's why I take psychology—and not just in the form of therapy,
But as one of my studies; I take psychology to understand myself. I have my own form of CBT;
Rationalising my negative thoughts, and providing a constant stream of positivity,

Because it will get better.
And while it does,
I will continue to work on my studies,
With everything I have.

Self-Love

Do you remember when you were ten?
Snot-nosed, and puffy-eyed,
You did not love yourself then.
You did not know how
To love yourself broken.

Fast forward to three years later:
On the brink of a new dawn,
When your peers began to see you;
Not the chair, nor the Cerebral Palsy
That hid, (and yet caused), the chronic depression
For those three years.

You felt like a newly hatched gosling;
All fluff and feathers,
Taking your first step into the sun.
And with the sun's help,
You discovered parts of yourself long forgotten;
Thought drowned in an ocean of sorrow and discontentment,
and unadulterated loathing for both self and body.
This sun, came to be known as self-love.

Fast forward once more,
To November 2015.
You came out to your parents as a transgender man;
The best decision you've ever made.

Oh, but, Eyal,
If you thought disability depression was tough,
Wait until you experience gender dysphoria, coupled with
depression, coupled with anxiety; the terrible triplets.

They will invade your privacy,
Come crawling into your bed next to you,
Make it hard to breathe;
Like your heart's a grenade,
Is only ever three seconds away
From imploding. And you don't want to think about what'll
happen if it does.
The truth is, you'd go through disability depression again to
avoid this.

Yet, the sun, the one you learnt to let
Shine on you at thirteen,
Is still there.
This is how you learned to love yourself broken.

And there is no comparison:
If you asked me to choose between being
An able-bodied woman or a disabled man,
I'd choose the latter in a heartbeat.

There is no comparison.
My disability is the least of my concerns right now.
And as I'm nearing the end of my gender evaluation,
It gets harder to deal with the anxiety and social dysphoria.

But, Eyar, I love you.
I love the girl you were, the man you are, and the greater man
you will be.
Life is messy,
But I love you—you are me.
I love myself,
I love myself,
I love, myself.
Learning to accept both my disability and gender identity has
made me a better person;
Has made me try to make the most of what I've got,
And I love myself in spite of everything I've ever been, or am
going through.

I know on the days when it's hard to like myself,
Hard to find equilibrium in me,
Somewhere, the sun of self-love
Will continue to burn,
As I embark on the rest of my life.
Never to be put out,
Again.

How Can I Thank You?

How can I thank you?
Tell me how.
I know the analogies of flying to the moon and back
Isn't going to cut it;
In fact, nothing's going to cut it;
Nothing encapsulates love or gratitude
Enough to be said sufficiently with words,
Nothing can ever begin to.

So tell me, how can I thank you?
I know I'm not the easiest person to deal with;
I try to deal with emotional turmoil alone, or get help from
others beside you,
So that there's a chance you won't have to deal with that too;
My disability's hard enough without the pain of my identity
crisis.

My dear family,
How on earth do I thank you for supporting my transition into
my authentic self?
You may be puzzled: you're still struggling with it,
Still confused,
Still wrapping your head round it,
So why would I thank you?
This is going to take some time, I know that.
But the knowledge that I am loved every step of the way is
enough to give me hope
For a better future.
So, I guess what I'm trying to say is,
Thank you for loving me, no matter what happens. I promise,
I will never let you down.

You See Me

I've always presented myself
Optimistically in public.
Always let that side of me prevail,
No matter the circumstances.
And while that side is genuine,
It's all people really see.
But you see me.

You know that I'm gasoline;
Know that I can burst into the flames of a breakdown
Much faster than anybody could imagine.
You know that I'm neurotic:
Know how my anxieties
Leave me gasping for air,
Unable to breathe.
You see me.

You know that I'm glue;
Trying to piece and hold myself together,
Like I know I can.
You know that I'm a people pleaser;
How I'd put the happiness of others before myself,
Which is one of the causes of my anxieties.
You see me.

You know that my brain
Transports me to the worst-case scenario
In most situations.
You know how I spend my time
Removing the gunk from my brain,
So that I catch sight of the light up ahead.

You know that I'm trying so hard to be myself;
To make my family comfortable
With me as their son, not daughter.
And, you know I will make it someday.

Mack, you know all of this
Because you see me.
Only one other person sees me in this depth:
My father.
You know how to help me teach him and anybody else about
my identity;
How to remind me it'll all be okay,
Despite the struggles,
So I can remind them of this.

You're an excellent rant partner!
You hear me without judgment;
No matter how irrational I am,
Then always help me back off the cliff edge;
Get my feet on solid ground.
Mack, I've told you things
Hardly anyone else knows about.
Putting up walls with you is futile;
You already see me.

You see me in all my messy, complicated glory;
The good and the bad.
Though I live in London,
And you live in Nashville,
I feel so safe when emailing and Skyping with you.
I'm completely myself with you;
There's nothing we can't talk about now.

There may be some things in this poem
That you didn't know about me.
But you will embrace these with open arms,
Because you embrace me. In my entirety.
Mack, my dear, dear friend,

I want to know you until my dying day.
But for now, all that's left for me to say,
Is thanks for seeing me.

Survive

My best friend and I made a pact.
Over Skype, we promised each other to keep going;
No matter how our demons attack us,
No matter how tempting a pistol may sound,
We promised to survive.

When my father tells me
That my chance of survival after birth was 40%,
I think of the times my will to survive
Was much less.
At its worst,
My will had a 0% chance of survival;
There was no hope.

I remember the familiar conversations
With my best friend about loosing
The will to live. We both know that pitfall too well. So, I
promised myself
That I would help us both bite the bullet,
Not surrender to it.
And as our friendship grew
Over all the stories, advice and turmoil we went through,
So did the strength of my promise.
We know we'll catch each other if we fall.
And we're strong enough to survive, no matter what—we
know that now.

As we make our pact,
My best friend watches me;
His eyes full of warmth and happiness.
'I promise.' He says.

'I promise too'. I say.
And with that, a deal is made.
We both smile;
We mean it.

RS Course

Miss Lauder said:
"The more you study Philosophy, the less you know."
As ironic as it sounds,
She's right.

At the start of the RS course,
I'm confident in my views about the world—
I have to be; the unknown scares me.

But then, slowly,
As we traverse our way round the twists and turns
Of the theories by Plato, Aristotle and Kant,
Applying the ethics of Bentham to Euthanasia,
I realise that I cannot be certain about everything:
There are many grey areas I didn't see before.
Mr Newman once told me it's okay
To have pieces that don't quite fit the puzzle—that's where
mindfulness comes in; to help smooth the rough edges.

"The more you study philosophy, the less you know."
And you know what? I'm okay with that;
I'm okay with not having the answers to every challenge I
face.
I'm okay with being confused, yet having the courage
To find the answers within myself.
I'm okay with acknowledging I'm a complicated person;

I have a lot of baggage.
I won't go into it now,
But studying philosophy and ethics has taught me how,

To claim my baggage and work through it—even if it gets
rocky.

So I wrote this poem,
To say thank you, Miss Lauder and Mr Newman,
For two incredible years of RS;
They've made me a better person.

Which, according to Aristotle's virtue ethics,
Is one step closer,
To achieving universal happiness.

For Miss Skipp

After thanking Miss Skipp for the umpteenth time,
She writes in an email:
"It has been an absolute pleasure to teach you this year! I am
only disappointed that I don't get to teach you sociology,"
And I smile.

When Miss Skipp teaches,
She always makes us think of ways to remember information,
And makes sarcastic jokes that only I seem to find amusing.

She has said that she's a big softy,
Even though she doesn't always show it.
This was evident to me
When I first came to thank her for all she had done during the
year:

Her eyes smiling with tenderness as I thank her,
As she sees a video of me walking,
As she tells me that I inspire her;
She says that I always make things seem easier
Than they must be. And that inspires her.

Miss Skipp always has a smile on her face;
Always finds a way to motivate students.
This, is what I admire;
This is a quality I have seen persist in every teacher I've ever
had.
Miss Skipp is no exception. I will always admire this quality.

On the days when she is down,
I can imagine her singing to "*The Sound of Music*",
And I smile once again.

It has been a privilege to be your student, Miss Skipp.
And if you're ever low, remember this quote:
"It never gets easier; you just get better."
Let these words restore your strength, as it does mine,
And in time, I guarantee your procedural memory
Will remind you how to smile again.

Scenario

Lying in bed.
At the intermission between sleeping and waking up,
I have a vision:

I'm at a school reunion.
Having made the transition into the man I truly am,
I'm the happiest version of myself.

Then, amongst the sea of people,
I see him. He looks exactly the same.
Contrary to my own expectations,
(For I'd always expected to be able to interact with him,
should we meet again),
My instinct tells me to run,
Tells me to hide,
Tells me to do whatever it takes to avoid him.

And in that moment,
I'm so grateful for my beard, voice, and anything else
That prevents him from making the link
Between me, and the girl whose privates he touched in year
six.

By this point,
I'm in a cold sweat.
I remember having the same reaction months
After the event happened.

And if I'm honest,
The event in year 6
Is the only cause of my reaction;

Our other history doesn't matter.

The scenario ends there.
I'm in bed, safe.
And I know I shouldn't still fear him.
The fact that I did, surprised me;
I haven't seen him in years,
And I've forgiven him for what he did.

Should this scenario ever occur,
Despite my instincts, I hope I don't run away; I want to
conquer the fear.
If we talk, I hope he won't recognise me,
If we talk, I shall be civil.
And only hope I'm too strong,
To ever let him hurt me again.

Cold Feet

I am terrified.
There's no other way to put it:
I am terrified.

I made a decision:
It's time to come out publicly;
To start the social transition into the man
I want everybody to see,
Time to show the world the real me.

Yet, I am terrified.
I'm standing on the cliff I'm meant to jump from,
With a severe case of cold feet.

There's a difference between everybody thinking
You're questioning your identity,
And telling them you're sure.

I always thought I'd be out of the closet the first chance I
could;
Take rocket boots and fly in a new sky.
But on the ground of this tall cliff,
It's a long way down.
Now, suddenly the closet is as inviting as it is suffocating;
I don't know what to do. I am terrified.

I can't stay closeted;
It's detrimental to my health.
But I don't know how to move,
Don't know how to jump,
Off the cliff.

I have nothing to fear;
I know that. But my anxiety
Isn't rational; it twists my stomach
Into knots so tight,
It's impossible to breathe.

I hear my mother's voice in my ear.
She said she would have accepted this a long time ago,
Had she believed it to be true.
I know I must do this, contrary to her wishes,
And hope she will catch up soon.
I've waited two years for her;
I don't think she even realises that,
But I do. I've felt every moment,
And who knows how long she'll take to accept me as her son?
I don't want to hurt her,
But now I need to do right by myself.

Yet, somehow,
I find myself standing at the edge of the cliff I'm meant to
jump from,
With a severe case of cold feet. I am terrified.
I'm terrified of being myself,
And I don't know why.

I know people will catch me,
Should I fall instead of fly.
And I can't stay here. It's detrimental to my health.
We are drawn to what we know;
But that doesn't mean we can't change.

I'm standing at the edge of the cliff I'm meant to jump from,
With a severe case of cold feet.
I am terrified.
But I need to learn how to jump.

Today

Today,
Is a new day.
With a new start
To my life.

Today,
All the social constraints,
The neurotic ticks in my brain,
Don't matter.

Today,
I'm singing Nina Simone's *'Feeling good'*
Very out of tune,
But meaning it.

Today,
I'm at peace.
I don't remember the last time I felt this way;
It's a wonderful feeling.
Anything's possible now.

Today,
Like a bird released from its cage,
I am free.
I finally jumped from the cliff;
The leap of faith paid off,
And today, I am free. I'm finally out of the closet, and free!

I'm free to be the man I never thought I could be.
I am surrounded by so much love,
It restores my confidence
That I'll be okay.

Coming out as a transman
Doesn't mean my life will be void of pain.
There's still a lot to overcome,
But being true to myself
Will make life easier.

So, Eyar,
Go ahead: write yourself the future
You never dreamed possible.
Because my future begins,
Today.

Voice

You're back.
After 5 years,
You hear I'm trying to gain equilibrium of self-confidence,
And you want to destroy it.

Well, have I got news for you:
I'm no longer your fool,
You won't win, and hold me captive
For the next three years,
Like you did when I was 10.

You will not make me
The enemy of myself;
You won't destroy my self-esteem,
You won't tell me I'm worthless,
I know better now. You have no power over me anymore,
I will defeat you before you do serious damage.

You mean nothing to me.
You're just a voice in my head;
And I stopped listening years ago.

You're not alone in my head,
There's another voice called cognitive positivity and self-love;
A voice designed to combat your lies,
To raise my self-esteem, not burn it to ashes.

I meant what I said in my self-love poem:
I love myself.
You can't tell me otherwise.

Tell me, what makes you think you can win?
You put up a good fight,
But I defeated you once, and I can do it again.
Do you really want to challenge me?
I'm much stronger than I was at 13.

I owe you thanks;
My experience with you helped me deal with
The issues surrounding my identity.
So, in the words of Christina Aguilera:
"Thanks for making me a fighter,"
Or rather, testing the fighter my father made me from birth.
Just because I'm vulnerable right now,
Doesn't make me weak.

You're nothing but a voice in my head.
And you're not welcome here. You never were.
There's no room for you anymore,
You have no power over me.

I will raise my self-confidence to a consistent level,
My cognitive positivity will remain.
I will defeat you, again.
However many times you decide to return,
I'll defeat you again and again,
Even if you bring anxiety and depression.
I know who I am now:

My name is Eyar Berman-Roth.
Are you ready for me?

Jigsaw Puzzle

Society is a jigsaw puzzle.
And I am an odd piece;
Never quite fit in.

Thinking about it,
It feels weird to be studying sociology;
Feels weird, considering I spent most
Of my adolescence wanting to conform to social norms,
Feels weird, considering I never could.

I'm a complex creature who,
Even when accepted by others, knows I'm an odd piece,
And probably always will be;
There's no point in hiding it.
It's taken me so long to be okay with this;
So long to be okay with the fact that I'm a little eccentric by nature,
And there's nothing wrong with that.

Here, I find myself studying sociology:
The study of society and its behaviour.
Discussing the social norms and constructs
I so frequently resist.
And though my peers and teachers are wonderful,
To me, under the circumstances, it's laughable.

The truth is,
I don't know my place in society;
I believe I have a place,
But I don't know what it is;
I hope I find it someday.

My poetry is a reflection of my soul.
Usually I would have an answer to the dilemma by now,
But I don't. This poem has no answer.

Society is a jigsaw puzzle.
And I'm an odd piece;
Never quite fit in.
But maybe society needs odd pieces,
To complete the puzzle.

Anxieties

Dad,
I know you want me to get over my phobia of films.
Know you think I'm being held back,
And that you don't want me missing out.
You can't understand why I don't want to look into curing it.

Dad, if you only knew,
How many anxieties I overcome every day.
How many monsters I slay,
How brave I must be just to keep on top of everything,
How, the fact that I am on top of everything,
Is sometimes nothing short of a miracle.

I know you know what it is to be scared;
But your questions about my phobia only makes things worse.
And I choose not to deal with this now,
Because I'm tired of dealing with anxieties;
Tired of fighting against so many obstacles,
You've been by my side all my life;
You know I deal with what I have to.

This is one of the least important,
But it causes the most intense anxiety,
Unlike any of my smaller fears.
And it's not like I haven't tried to get over it—I've watched
many films I'd never dreamt I could watch,

But I can't shake this phobia.
I don't want to look into curing my phobia of films right now;
I'm scared of facing it,
And it's one less thing to think about.

If I'm ever ready to look into curing it with professional help,
I will.

So, Dad,
I know you mean well.
I know you're trying to help,
But please, let it go.

University Feelings

Everybody wants me to go to university.
Everybody.
But I'm not sure.

There are so many feelings I have,
So many ticks in my brain
That drive me insane,
So much anxiety about the prospect of university;
It makes me sick.

Some of these feelings are expected;
The fear of debt for instance.
But I know this can be overcome.

I would not prevent myself from going
For this reason alone,
But the source of the anxiety is far too complex to put into
words;
The edges get stuck in my throat,
I get tongue-tied every time I try to explain it.

When I tell people I'm not sure about university,
They tell me I should go.
Think that "it's written all over me",
Think that my intelligence makes me destined for it.
This does not help.
I don't want to go.
I don't want to go;
I get that surprises most people,
But that doesn't change the truth! Only a few people
understand this!

My parents worry that not going will limit my potential;
That having a degree will improve my credentials,
Especially as I'm physically limited.

I thought I heard the underlying disappointment as my father says:
"Don't go to uni." Turns out, he wants me to make my own choice.
But, don't get me started on what my mother thinks.
I don't want to disappoint anyone. I care too much about what others think;
I've always worked hard for the sake of everybody's expectations,
Either that, or as a distraction from my problems. I've never really worked for my sake;
Maybe that's why every acceptance letter feels like a ten-foot drop for my stomach;
I know I really don't want to do this.

The truth is,
I'm having a panic attack as I write.
I'm quaking in my chair;
I realise I have good potential,
But I'm not keen about university.
And I know I tend to overthink things,
But everything about uni feels wrong.
The truth is,
University will metaphorically kill me
From the pressure and all that is required,
Just like my A-levels almost do.

And considering I've no desire to study,
I don't want to go through with it. It's not worth it.
Nothing is confirmed,
But I'm hoping for something else.
Anything else.
Until then, I'm trying to alleviate this fear;
Find some direction in life.

This poem (if you can call it that) is nothing but word-vomit;
There is no structure,
No rhyme or reason;
Just like my feelings.

I'm keeping my options open,
But I can't help hoping,
That university remains my last.

Self-Confidence

I ask him what he sees in me.
He's one of the only people to know the darkest parts of me.
I ask him what he sees in me.

Having self-confidence is a gift;
And, looking at me on a stage,
I could pull the wool over your eyes;
If I need to do something for someone else,
I have all the confidence in the world;
I must do a good job for whoever or whatever I'm
representing.

But the truth
Is I can get so aloof
When it comes to me. Everything I could ever say
Dissolves. And I swallow. Hard.

I remember when,
At the age of ten,
A nervous breakdown with depression
Rendered me hostage, destroyed every ounce
Of confidence and self-esteem I ever had.
And later,
Once I managed to re-kindle the flame of self-love, bringing
back my self-esteem,
My self-confidence also restored but continued to fluctuate.

I've been through a lot since then,
But still always struggle to find equilibrium with self-
confidence.
Irrational as it may seem,

I see greatness in others, but not me.

For years,
My father had no self-confidence.
He doesn't want this to be passed
Down the family tree, so,
Every time he sees it in me,
He reminds me to be the best I can be,
But it's hard to talk about my problems.

In an email to one of my closest friends,
I ask him what he sees in me.
There's no secrecy between us,
He knows everything;
He's one of the only people I'm completely open with,
The only person I find it easy to talk to about anything—
It's always been different with him; everything comes easy,
even when it's hard.

I ask him what he sees in me.
And as he lists my qualities,
I know I should believe him;
He's never lied to me.

"I believe you," I tell him.
Because maybe this is the only way,
To start fixing this.

Ode to Shark Week (My Period)

Why are you here?
Don't answer that, we both know what you'll say.
You're the natural occurrence;
A reminder of the situation
I never asked to be in.

My uterus hates me.
You are the product of that hate;
Flowing angry red in my underwear,
You love to make me bleed.

It's not your fault.
You're just doing what comes naturally,
You're more than happy to remind me of my anatomy,
Not that I need reminding.

My gender dysphoria's worse with you,
I need reminding that some boys get periods too;
Your existence doesn't make me any less of a man.
And with this, I do what I can,
To distract myself. To ignore the anxiety and desire to self-
destruct.

When you're here, I can't speak;
Most of the time I weep.
And I can't help feeling weak,
Because I'm a fragile creature;

A creature whose tears are raindrops,
Creating streams down my face,
That sometimes turn into waterfalls.

How is it
That you flow so freely,
And my emotions are too painful
To be expressed? Even when I don't cry,
Even when I try to hold myself together,
Everything still hurts.

Though I'm out of the closet,
My body remains the same,
And there's nothing to blame.
This may not be your fault,
But it's not mine either!
You may be the natural occurrence,
But I can't deal with you, or the dysphoria you cause.
My dreams of a body that fits my identity,
Are dreams still.

There's a reason you're called shark week:
Your bite and dysphoria cause too much pain,
To be called anything else.

Seasons

I was born in spring.
Like a flower, I was given the chance to bloom;
Blossomed in the morning light
Of a care-free childhood,
Saw the beauty and innocence in everything.

Summer is warm and bright:
I was taught to harness these qualities,
Allow sunbeams to shine from me;
Make the day as joyful as possible
For me and everybody else,
Like a summer's day.

Autumn is my favourite season:
There's beauty even in change.
We're a diverse, complex, colourful species,
Inside and out. But we're beautiful!
Like leaves, we're blown in different directions
From where we came from,
Leading us to develop;
No two roads are ever the same, so,
Sometimes our colours change too.
Maybe, like leaves, the different colours in a person tells the
story of where they've been;

Like how sometimes, when we're not looking,
We end up in winter.
I'm no stranger to the darkness;
No stranger to how winter occurs in May.
And you wonder where the sun is,
Or why it's darker and colder

In your own head than in December.
But if you keep looking, you might end up in

June 2016: I met the person I now call my best friend.
He turned my winter into spring in an instant;
Helped me re-build my soul,
Watched me blossom again into a new flower;
A better flower.
He makes me feel like there's rainbows coming out of my butt;
A feeling I only have with few people.
Our friendship is like the sun in summer,
Shining bright in everything we are.
I wouldn't change a thing.

Our lives are like seasons;
We rise and fall,
But get the opportunity to start the cycle over again.

The calendar says: December 2017.
I love seeing the lights at Christmas;
There's hope even in the darkness,
Always remember that.
Merry Christmas!

Next to This Christmas Tree

Sit with me,
Next to this Christmas tree,
Because it's too small to sit under.

Sit with me.
Let it be just the five of us;
Put all troubles aside,
Let them sleep for the day,
And enjoy each other's company.

On this Christmas day,
Please, sit with me.
You are all my greatest gift;
Anything else is a bonus.

Sit with me,
Next to this Christmas tree.
My dear family,
I hope your smiles light up the world;
I want to see you happy.

As we sit together
Next to this Christmas tree,
Know that I love you,
With everything I have and am.
To know that you love me in the same way,
Is enough.

New Year's Promise

I've spent the last few weeks
Floating adrift in a pool of anxiety;
Fretting over studies, gender dysphoria and the future,
Asking: "What on earth do I do next?"

But then,
I try to remember the good moments of 2017;
How brave I've been. How much courage it took
To endure the eight months of gender therapy with my
parents,
After a year-and-a-half of my family's confusion.

How free I felt on August 20th,
When a friend helped me find the strength
To come out publicly.
No more hiding. Live authentically.

I hold onto these moments like dreams;
Harnessing their light like a dream catcher,
So that my stream of positivity
Will remind me that I'll be okay;
That I'll work through my troubles,
And that I can do this.

Overall, 2017 was a great year.
And I latch on to this,
As my heart trembles in my hand.

I breathe deeply;
Allowing my lungs to be grateful for the taste of air.
My heart may be trembling, but it's beating;
I'm still here.

I know what people want for me.
But now, it's my turn!
And now, on the dawn of 2018,
I promise you, Eyar,
To do what feels right.
I've no idea what'll happen this year,
But if all else fails,
At the very least, Eyar, I'll do what feels right.

You can't please everyone,
So please yourself.
Grab 2018 by the horns,
And own it.

To Anyone Who May Date My Friends

To anyone who may date my friends:

You, are a very lucky person.
If you date my friends,
You need to know that
You, are a very lucky person.

You should also know that
My friends are crazy in the best possible way;
We always have crazy ideas like,
Thinking about catapulting paint onto school buildings or,
Being dared to shower in tomato juice and peanut butter!
They're always up for a laugh,
And always leave me in stitches!

My friends are wonderful:
They have great advice,
Which may come in handy during your relationship,
They'll stand by you—no matter what happens.

If you date my friends,
I hope you fall in love with them.
I hope you fall for their eyes;
Big beautiful spheres filled with sincerity,
And a lust for life that is infectious.

I hope you fall for their smile;
Which I hope will brighten your day
As much as it brightens mine.

I hope you fall for their sense of humour;
It is hard to describe what constitutes it,
But you'll understand when you meet them.
I hope you fall for their personalities;
My friends have such beautiful souls,
It's not hard to get to know them.
I hope you fall for everything about them.

I hope you're able to give yourself to them wholeheartedly,
And love them for everything they are.
'Cause there will be times when they will need you;
On the rough days, they will need you to be there for them.
I guarantee they'll be there for you, should you put trust in
them.

If you want to date my friends,
You should be open to anything;
Being this open helps them embrace
The complexity of the world.
One of my friends is polyamorous,
So if you're up for that—great!

If you date my friends,
You may meet me;
I will show you the best parts of my friends
So you never forget how you feel around them.
Addendum: my friends have also entrusted me to be their
wingman;
To get the ball rolling.
There's a possibility that you may briefly meet me
When you first meet them,
So, I apologise in advance if I use any lines from "How I Met
Your Mother",
Or don't have the best introduction lines in general,
But I promise they're worth it!

If you date my friends,
Please don't try to hurt them.

They deserve the same happiness you do.
They know I'm here for them when they fall,
But please don't break their hearts.

Like I said,
If you date my friends, you're a lucky person.
And I'm a lucky man,
To have them as friends.

Wish You Were Here

I really miss you, my friend.
I wish you were here.
But we have never met in person,
And are yet to break the distance.

You live in Nashville,
I live in London.
We're able to communicate through
Emails and YouTube and Skype,
Which I'm so grateful for;
But right now, I wish you were here.

I love our Skype calls;
Despite a 6-hour time difference,
We can spend hours talking to each other;
Just a couple of guys having a great time!

And I love that you let me give you 'Skype hugs',
It's the closest I can get to the real thing, for now.
Our friendship, and the bond we have,
Knows no distance.
But right now, I wish you were here.

We've been through so much together,
And you're one of the best friends I've ever had;
I'm so grateful to know you, and all you've done for me.
In my first ever poem to you,
I said catching the next flight to see you was easier than the
things we went through.
That statement will always be true,
But that doesn't mean that what we have to do

To be in the same vicinity is easy;
As I said, we've been friends for a long time, and are yet to break the distance.
Right now, I wish you were here.

We love each other like brothers.
The day you told me I could be
Part of your chosen family,
I was filled with a happiness
No words can describe.
I love you, Mack. We are family now. We are family now,
And I can't wait to be an uncle to your future adopted children!
But right now, I wish you were here.

I really miss you, Mack.
I really wish you were here.
Sometimes the 4,183 miles between us
Gets to me. And I'm sorry.
I should be used to this;
Most of my extended family live in Israel.

But that doesn't make this any easier;
Sometimes I miss you so much, it hurts!
I really wish you were here.
I want to hug you. Actually hug you.
You're one of the people who knows me best,
And I wish we weren't so far away from each other.

If it was easy for me to travel to you,
We both know I'd fly as soon as possible;
Wouldn't even think twice.
It's easier and cheaper for you to come here, though.
I wish you were here.

I know you'll visit England one day,
We've talked about it;
We will break the distance.

And until that day, I'll wait with you, Mack,
For as long as it takes.

Stages

In life, we move through different stages;
Each one important in their own way.

When I first came out to my parents as a transgender man,
I tried to let you go.
Thought I couldn't hold on to you,
The girl I was, and still become the man I am.

I wrote you a poem.
It was called '*Don't ask me to tell you I don't love you*'.
In it, I tried to bid you farewell,
Told you I couldn't keep you even though I love you.
You, the sacrifice,
You, who did nothing wrong.
Trying to say goodbye felt like pushing you out the window,
And I'm sorry if I ever caused you pain;
You didn't deserve it.
But I did what I thought was best at the time;
And in doing so, I grieved for you, too.

Things have changed since then:
Despite all the adieus, you never left.
I began to realise you didn't have to;
You were a stage in my life.
A stage I could move on from,
But didn't have to abandon.

You are a part of me, and always will be.
Now, as I live my life as the man I am—
Eyar, the man,
I'm happy to have moved on from your stage.

You, here in my heart.
I love you, you know that.
You'll always be an important part of me.
But, in giving myself the chance to be free,
I moved on to a different stage.

My Anxiety Speaks to Me

My anxiety speaks to me:
Hey, lover,
It's me. I know I'm an
Unwanted guest, but you'll
Let me in, right? No? No matter:
I'll just kick your door down instead!

Hey, lover,
How do you feel?
Have I
Caused your heart to race? Do you sweat? Can you
Feel me? Can you feel,
The affect I have on you? Do you,
Feel my presence?

Hey, lover,
Take a vacation.
Vacate this body;
Let me
Take control. I can pull your strings
Like a puppet. Love you so hard,
You can't breathe. Or function.
But that's okay, 'cause you're not here,
Are you?

Hey, lover,
Why don't we invite my cousin,
Depression, in too? After all,
Two guests are better than one,
Right? The more the merrier! I love
Making you borderline-depressed,

And we both love a drop in your mental health;
It's how we thrive!

Hey, lover,
Don't try and run from me. I'm
Right behind you. You can't escape,
'Cause I make you too weak;
Too weak and exhausted to complete school work efficiently,
And even more anxious when more work is added;
I can make you so anxious,
It's as if you can feel the neurons firing in your brain.
In other words, I win!! And I love it!!

I love how,
I can puncher your self-esteem;
Clog your throat, so that you
Can't speak the whole truth to most people,
And you'll believe the lies I tell you.

Hey, Eyar,
Sweetheart, don't cry:
You're not well, but I'm here. Let me
Stay here.
I won't hurt you. Let me
Wrap you in my arms.
I promise, I won't let go, for a long time.

Emotional Dependency

Emotional dependency is something
I wish I lived without.
It's hard enough being physically dependent;
Hard enough relying on others to do things
So many take for granted: going to the toilet or showering, for
instance.
The last thing everyone needs is for me to be emotionally
dependant.

And yet,
I find myself in this situation once again.
Today, my gender dysphoria is yet again a tyrant;
Is yet again unpredictable,
Is yet again a reminder that I don't feel welcome in a body
I'm meant to call home,
Is yet again a reminder that my identity crisis was far more
turbulent than accepting my disability could ever be.

I can't stand being emotionally dependent.
But today, I'm gasoline;
I'm so emotionally unpredictable,
I can't help but blow up into a burning blaze of fire and tears;
I can't control myself,
And calling on my friends to help feels like saying:
"I know I was fine last week, but now I'm dynamite!"
On the verge of imploding in on myself again,
And I wish I didn't need them. I don't want to need them, or
my family, like this.
It's hard enough to be physically dependent.

Whoever I'm dependent on, they always come through.
And they know I'd do the same for them too.
I know I'm never alone,
I just wish I didn't need help finding my way home.

Name

I must own myself.
I will own myself.
Starting with my name.

It's hard enough owning
My own body. As I write this poem,
I'm battling the depths of depression again.
Trying to find hope that, one day, I will medically transition
from female-to-male;
Trying to find hope that I can own myself.

My name has Israeli heritage.
It is my birth name. It is gender neutral.
It is a name that I love and identify with but,
When one of my sisters and my mother criticise my
pronunciation of my own name,
Call it insulting,
Maybe they were overreacting,
Maybe it was a spur of the moment;
A one-time thing,
But I tell them I have the right to own my name.

I'm sorry if my name doesn't roll off my tongue
In the way you want it to.
When my mother finally cradled me in her arms as an infant,
No doubt she knew what she wanted me to be.
I tried everything to be the perfect child for her,
But never could; I feel like I'm everything she doesn't want
me to be.
In my transition from female to male,

I choose to keep my birth name. If I'd wanted to change my name, I would have.

My mother says this is the name I was given.
This is true, but that doesn't mean I can't choose how to own it.
Since I was eight, my mother claims to have 'made a mistake' with the legal spelling of my name.
She now spells my name with 'I' instead of 'E', despite my objections,
Claims it's the 'correct' way to spell it,
But this just messes up other people's pronunciation of my name.

My name is Eyar. It is spelled E-y-a-r and pronounced as if it was written E.R. This is what I tell people.
This is how I choose to own MY name. I won't change anything about that. But, I still like the Hebrew pronunciation of it.

When one of my sisters and my mother
Criticise my pronunciation of my own name,
My depression makes me feel worthless.
Makes me feel that I can't own myself;
I'm always just out of my own reach.

I write this poem in my bedroom;
It's the room I feel safest in.
It's seen all versions of me;
Heard all my thoughts and cries without judgement,
Lets me be 100% me without ever complaining,
Just like the few people I call home.

I remind myself I have worth.
I remind myself that I can overcome this depression,
As I've done so many times before.
That I will own my body someday.

I know I'm a man, even though my body and mother disagree right now.
It may be a long wait, but I'll get to where I want to be.

I must own myself.
I will own myself.
And it starts by owning my name.

Push

Depression is an invisible pathogen;
Consumes you from the inside,
Makes you so ill, you lose yourself;
Find yourself searching for something you know you lost
somewhere in the darkness;
That piece of yourself that
You can't find right now.

People tell me I'm ill when I have a common cold.
Oh, how little they know.
A common cold is nothing in comparison.
Depression is an invisible pathogen;
No one can see it unless the host wants them to,
And that in itself can be terrifying.

I have been ill with depression enough times to know,
That not pushing back will make me far worse.
But that's just the problem.
Sitting here,
Depression drains every ounce of energy in me;
I've not yet had the strength to push back.
This is what my depression wants;
Wants to lie to me, wants to make me weak,
Wants to drag me down further into the abyss of black,
But I know I must push against my demons;
It's the only way I'll find the light again.

Eyar, can you hear me?
I know you're there,
I caught a glimpse of you today
During a mindfulness session.

I still can't see you right now,
But I've made the fog translucent
Enough to know you're there.
Hang on, dude! I'm coming!

I must push myself up.
I must fight this depression.
Enough with the self-harm thoughts,
Enough with the rough nights,
Enough with the questioning of worth,
I know I'm worth something!

I will take up my jousting lance,
Attach it to my wheelchair,
And drive straight through depression with it;
Keep pushing through until it's slain,
And I can breathe again.
I will find you, Eyar! This I swear!

A friend reminds me
That breathing is good for my health,
So, I'll allow its nourishment
To give me the strength to trump this depression.
All I have to do,
Is push.

When (After "If" by
Rudyard Kipling)

When I first read your poem at 13,
I don't believe I fully understood it;
It was the first poem I found under the search 'Inspirational
poetry' for an English project,
My mind too naive to comprehend
The significance of such utterances,
I know I didn't understand what you meant.

When I read those same words now,
I'm filled with a burning hope
That it's possible to keep going.
It's clear we've both had our fair share
Of turbulence.
I have read those words a thousand times now,
And I will read them a thousand more.

When I have my patience tested
By life's waiting game,
When I lose my faith,
I use your poem
To remind my spirit to rise
Against the unforgiving minute,
And run for at least sixty seconds;
The start is always the hardest part,
The biggest leap.
And the final stretch before the end goal can be just as
gruelling,
But in both cases,
Even the worst minute is only 60 seconds;

It may get easier after that.

Kipling, now when I read your poem "If",
I understand what you mean.
And I'm trying to follow in your footsteps;
My will is holding on,
To be a man we'd both admire.

You may have died,
But your words are timeless.
So when I say thank you, Kipling,
Know I mean it.

April Birthdays

Congratulations! It's your birthdays,
And this is your crazy joint birthday present poem!

Mum calls my youngest sister a lamb (amongst various other names),
And looking at her mass of golden curls,
It may be appropriate to call her a golden lamb;
Each curl representing rays of the sun.
Somehow, it's fitting you were both born in April:

Spring is the season of new life.
And, Mum, I may not know much;
Still have a lot to learn,
But I've observed,
That since bringing both my sisters into this world,
The new lease of life that it gave you
Is reflected in your bond.

To my youngest sister:
You're thirteen now. I still remember when I held you on my
lap on Mum's birthday—you were one day old,
Which now makes me feel old. I'm so proud of you!
And I want to pay to see you in the West End one day!

And no, Mum, you're not old,
Even though you think you are,
So we'll act like you're getting younger!
I know we don't get along,
But I'm proud of you, too.

I want to buy you an owl, I know how you love them;
You can call him Brian,
And go goo-goo over his eyes!

Both of you, on your birthdays,
Be happy. Let your smiles mirror the morning sun;
We're in spring after all!
I love you both so much!
Happy birthday!

Stay

Eyar, you must stay.
You must stay.

My mental health
Has derailed again.
Has taken a turn for the tragic;
I feel like dying again.

My gender dysphoria, anxiety and depression are relentless,
merciless beasts;
I feel like I'm already dying.
I can't control myself,
I can't breathe.

I'm on fire!
I'm on fire in a body that betrays me daily.
Just when you think you've beaten your demons,
They return for your soul;
Eyes bloodshot-thirsty with vengeance, and I,
I don't recognise myself anymore.
It's been a turbulent two months,
And I'm suicidal.

You know what's the worst thing about this?
I want to die at the same time as not wanting to die at all;
My depression, anxiety and dysphoria commands
My mind to produce suicidal thoughts;
Tries to convince me that this is the way to end the pain, but

At the same time, I know I don't really want to die;
I've been here before, and I know it must get better somehow,

Just as it did before.
This paradox is utterly terrifying;
I'm so scared.
Eyar, you must stay.

You must stay.
I called a hotline today;
Told the person on the other end
How I feel. And yet, acknowledged I'll be okay,
Even though I don't feel that way.
All I have now is tunnel vision into endless black.

But the sun continues to shine even when we can't see it,
right?
It's always darkest before the dawn, right?
I deserve to live, right?

Remember the pact.
Remember the pact you made with Mack,
How you both agreed to survive times like these;
You know that pact's keeping you alive right now.
Mack is living proof that this will get better;
He's come so far in his medical transition from female-to-
male,
And you know one day you will too,
You better believe it!

Remember your family and friends.
Remember how much you're loved;
Everyone sees so much hope and worth in you.
It'd kill them if you left.

Remember that you're alive;
Let every breath you take remind you
That your heart still beats.
You're not done here,
You're not even close to being done here,
And you know it.

There's so much to live for!
You can do this! I promise, it'll get better!
It must get better!

I'm suicidal.
But no matter what, I can't give up;
This isn't over.
Eyar, you must stay.
Eyar, you deserve,
To stay.

Reason

I cannot attend the prom for the end of sixth form.
This is unusual for me,
I'm known to love social occasions.
But I cannot attend the prom.
If people ask me why, I explain it's a family occasion.

I won't tell them about the last three months.
Won't tell them about my mental health;
How my gender dysphoria set me afire,
Lit me up in a burning blaze that caused too much
Smoke to see anything clearly.

I won't tell them about the depression and anxiety;
Won't tell them about the black,
Won't tell them about the noise;
The noise of my own thoughts,
Like a cyclone in my head.
Won't tell them how I could feel myself going insane;
How I could almost feel the neurons firing in my brain,
From my anxiety.

I won't tell them about April;
Won't tell them about the worst of it.
Won't tell them that month was shaped
Like the object I wish to forget.

I won't tell them how I blamed my exhaustion entirely on the
pressure of my academic studies;
This was only half the story.
Won't tell them how I narrowly avoided a nervous
breakdown,

But that was way too close for comfort.

I won't tell them about the social isolation.
Won't tell them how the only three people
I was comfortable talking to, were my father and two of my
closest friends.
Won't tell them that I literally forced myself to go out,
So my buddies from my development program would get paid
for working with me.
Won't tell them how I don't want to be in school,
But never used mental health problems as a reason to be
absent.

I won't tell them about my father.
Won't tell them about the times he held me, his son,
Tight in his arms as I lost my composure.
Won't tell them I'm too exhausted to take counselling again;
I'd rather pull through this without it.

I won't tell them I'm recovering;
They don't need to know this,
My behaviour's no different.
I tell them I have a family occasion.
This is no word of a lie,
But I won't tell them that asking my father
For a low-key celebration for graduation was a feat.
I may be recovering, but I can't be around people at prom
right now;
And whilst the idea of wearing a tux instead of a dress
Is so wonderful, I still can't go;
There'll be other chances to wear a tux.
I may be recovering, but I can't be around people at prom
right now;
It's too overwhelming.

If people ask me why I'm not coming to prom,
I tell them I have a family occasion.
That's the only reason they need to know.

For Meggie

Meggie,
You are one of the highlights of this academic year;
Knowing you is a joy.
I knew we'd get closer from being together more often,
But never could've anticipated this.

I love it when you talk to me;
Whenever you get excited about something,
You start yelling and bouncing with such gusto,
I can't help but smile.
Granted, there are times you know I have no idea what you're
talking about,
But you thank me for listening anyway.

And don't get me started on our Skype messages;
We send each other random videos,
And you introduce me to bisexual icons,
Not to mention, the women who are most likely to destroy you
with their attractive faces!
All these women seem to have slightly murderous traits, such
as Missy from 'Doctor Who'.
And we both know I cannot save you!

And I love how, 'cause you're cute,
No one expects you to be mischievous,
But you are! Not to mention all the puns you make;
Your witty humour's so great,
It's impossible to exaggerate how much we laugh,
Especially during our three-way Skype calls with Mack!

You know my catchphrase is 'yay';
Sometimes we get into the habit of yelling 'yay' to each other
Non-stop for a full five minutes,
Before bursting into laughter.

This is a crazy poem.
Meggie, you bring out the crazy in me!
And just like the rest of my friends,
You help me embrace my weirdness;
You don't mind it.
And you help calm some of my anxiety;
Our least favourite beverage!

You said I'm like an older brother to you;
A statement that touched me deeply.
You know that you're like a sibling to me;
A label that fits your gender fluid identity,
So I call you 'sib' for short.

Meggie, as I leave school this year,
You tell me I have nothing to fear;
I'll be okay.
We'll keep in touch.
So this isn't goodbye,
Just, see you soon, friend!

I'm Okay

I'm okay. I'm okay, but I've been better.
I've been better than this.
This chronic muscle pain's been here since June;
Almost three months, to be exact.
But, I'm okay.

I'm okay because I've been through worse;
Had worse pain than this.
Managed worse pain than this;
On my pain scale, this is about 7.5.
I don't use 10 very often;
My pain threshold is very high.
And, like I said, I've been through worse than this;
I've managed a few 10's, so I can manage a 7.5.
That's why I'm okay.

You see, I manage my Cerebral Palsy every day.
I manage the muscle tension every day;
You learn to live with it,
Learn to find ways to make it easier.
And if, on the rare occasion, the pain becomes chronic,
Well, I manage that too.
I'm okay, but I've been better.

The hardest part about having chronic muscle pain,
Isn't the pain,
But how it affects my body:

How it's even more difficult than usual to perform simple
tasks, such as driving my chair or writing this poem.

How sometimes, I can't move at all; the pain's at best when staying still, so I sit stuck, until I can bring myself to move my arm again. And when I can, each move is slow and painful.

How I have more spasms than usual, so my movements are often erratic.

How sometimes, my diaphragm muscles are so tight, I can't breathe.

How for almost three months, I've had 24-hour pain, top to toe.

How nothing I do seems to work right now. In fact, it's getting worse.

And how I'm so exhausted from everything. Even though there's been days I can barely do anything, I'm still exhausted.

I've hardly told anyone about this.
I don't want people to know,
I don't want people to see me in pain,
Don't want them to see me coping;
There are very few people whom I'm comfortable sharing this with.
You see, I cope with the frustration, too;
Have breakdowns in the privacy of my bedroom,
Where no one else can see,
And no one else knows what's going on.
I'm okay, but I've definitely been better.

The Decision

You did the right thing.
You know you did.
There's no regrets about that decision;
It was right at the time.

You did the right thing.
You know you did.
It was a turbulent time,
And making that decision was tumultuous too;
Was no walk in the park,
A classic battle of head and heart,
But you did the right thing.

You made the right decision.
You did the right thing.
You had your reasons, so you kept the decision private;
A secret agreement between you and yourself,
You promised you'll find an alternative.

You did the right thing.
You know you did.
There's no regrets about that decision.
Still you find yourself, many months later, thinking about it;
What might've happened if you chose differently.
After all, you wanted to choose differently,
Would've given anything to choose differently,
But you didn't. And you made the right decision.

There's no regrets about that decision;
It was right at the time.
You did the right thing.
Even if nobody else knows it.

Dear Future Vet

Dear future vet,
I'm so proud of you.
You, my little sister. Even though you're only sixteen,
You know what you want.

Dear future vet,
Do you remember the pigeon you called Colin?
You and dad helped nurse his broken leg,
And with tears in your eyes, you buried him when he passed
away.
That's when I knew you're going to be one great vet!

Dear future vet,
Please expect me to visit you at your practice;
If you want me to find an excuse, I'll borrow the neighbour's
dog,
Or pretend I've turned into an excessive cat person,
And bring ten sick cats to you,
Even though I'm not that keen on cats… or hedgehogs,
But don't tell our pets that!

I just want to see you work;
Want to see your eyes light up
The way they do when you care for our pets.
I suspect you'll also have three cats and maybe a Chihuahua,
too!
I want to see you happy.

Dear Maya,
You'll be a wonderful vet;
You care about animals so much!

And we both know it's going to be a lot of work,
But if this is what you want, go for it! I believe in you!

I know you're not a vet yet,
But I'm so proud of you! And I love you so much!
And maybe one day, I'll be able to gladly say,
That my sister is now a vet!

Why I Choose Not to Drink

In England, the legal drinking age is eighteen.
On my 18th birthday, everyone I knew offered me a drink. I politely declined.
I've still never consumed alcohol.
I often get confused looks when I say I don't drink, nor have any intention of drinking. People say I'm better off without it, But can't stifle their confusion at my reluctance to consume any alcohol.
There are two reasons why I choose not to drink:

The first, is that I do not want the effect of alcohol:
I don't want the tipsiness, the hangover, the nausea, the vomiting, the lowered inhibitions, the decline in balance and perception,
I don't want any of that. I'm fine seeing the effect of alcohol on others, but I don't want it on me.
I've had some of these effects from pain-killers nurses used to give me after surgeries. I hated it! And let's not get started on the more severe effects taught in school!
So, in short, the first reason is because I'm deterred by it. It's the reason I give when asked why I don't want to drink.

The second reason,
The second reason… is more severe.
The second reason… is harder to digest,
Is harder to spit out my mouth,
Lies dormant in me, waiting to see if I'll reveal it.
The second reason I choose not to drink,
Is because part of me worries I won't be able to stop:

The only circumstance where I'm not deterred by alcohol,
Is when my mental health's declined.
Alcohol can be used as a depressant drug.
And I've lost count of the number of times I've thought of using alcohol to drown my feelings.

If I start drinking,
I may open the floodgates;
Maybe not in the first instance,
But at some point.

If I start drinking,
Part of me worries that, on that rare occasion
When alcohol isn't deterring,
I will drink to oblivion;
Will use it as an excuse,
A method of self-destruction;
Destroy myself from the inside.
So, I stay sober,
Even when my mind lies and tells me drinking is a solution.

I know drinking doesn't have to turn into alcoholism or oblivion,
But since I only desire to drink during mental health problems,
I choose not to drink;
Don't start what I may not be able to stop,
Don't need another potential method of harm,
That's not the way to do things.

There are two reasons why I choose not to drink:
The first is because I'm genuinely deterred by it.
And if I'm not,
The second is because I want to live.

Brain Fog

I don't know how I feel.
I don't know what my brain's doing.

This isn't depression,
This isn't anxiety,
This isn't helped by my gender dysphoria,
And it's super weird.

This, is what I'm calling 'brain fog';
So called because it feels like a layer of thick, dense fog now
presses on my brain,
Makes it heavy,
Short-circuit's the messages, and
My gender dysphoria's a catalyst for this;
There are so many conflicting messages
From the fog, dysphoria and cognitive positivity,
It all sounds like white noise;
Hissing and crackling in my brain,
It's too loud.

I know this isn't depression;
I'm still able to think positively
About the good things in my life,
And that makes me happy.

But when there's no distractions,
The brain fog suddenly transports me to a dark place,
Transports me to the edge, where I question whether I can pull
through the dysphoria,
Even though I know I can;
I don't want to think about the edge!

Right now, I have brain fog.
The dense fog presses down on my brain,
Making it heavy.
I don't know how I feel right now,
The fog's confusing my thoughts and emotions;
I don't know what my brain's doing,
I don't know how to lift the fog.

Only one other person knows about the brain fog;
I don't like sharing my problems,
But he's the exception.
He knows how messed up I can be,
I tell him everything.
And he's always so good to me,
We often exchange advice with each other;
His is helpful even if he doesn't know how to help,
Even if we both don't know how to solve the problem.

I ask my brain how to make it feel better;
I ask my brain how to lift the fog,
And it says,
Nothing.

For My Father

Dad,
I'm sorry it took me so long to write this poem;
Despite years of being a poet,
I was always at a loss for the right words.
But now I'm going to try.

You may have missed my birth,
But you've made up for it, more than tenfold!
'Cause since day three,
You've always been there for me.

You gave me an active childhood;
No doubt you remember the monkey bars, the football,
Or how you attached scooter handles to my skateboard, so I
could keep my balance when riding it—we called it my
'scooter-board'. And it was awesome!
You always find a way to make the seemingly impossible,
possible;
Something that never ceases to amaze me.
Dad, you made me feel invincible!
And I know I didn't appreciate it as a child,
But I do now;
My childhood was one of the greatest gifts you've given me,
And I'll never forget it!

Your army unit was called 'The Flying Tigers'.
You'd tell me stories about the trials of your service,
And you always call me your 'little tiger';
Tell me that tigers are more resilient than lions,
And the resilience that you see in me,
Means I must be a tiger;

Born to be a fighter!

But, on the days I don't feel like fighting,
On the days that are black, and I can't track down
A way to face my demons,
You're always there.
Dad, you never leave me,
Even when I think you ought to.
You help me open up,
But you also listen when I say I need to handle it myself.
You're one of the people who will never judge me,
You're one of the people to remind me of my worth
When I don't feel good enough.
I know I'm a complicated person,
But you've always stuck by me. You've no idea how much
that means to me.

We've had our fair share of fights;
You know I'm almost as stubborn as you,
And you know that I find it easier to share
Some things with others than with you,
But you tell me that's okay.
And, at the end of the day,
I know I can always come to you;
There's never a taboo topic in sight.

Do you remember that time at one of my appointments at the
gynaecologist,
When my anxiety and gender dysphoria was sky-high,
And you told someone you have a son and two daughters?
It was the first time you'd said that,
And one of the best things you've ever said!
I didn't even care that the woman didn't know you were
talking about me,
I felt validated at the gynaecologist! You always know how
to make me feel better!

Dad,

I love you so much! You never get annoyed that I tell you this every day,

And you always appreciate what I have to say, and the ways I try to make the family's day a little bit easier.

I don't know if the patience learnt from growing up

On your parents' farm has anything to do with this,

But I've a feeling you were meant to be my father;

You're truly the best father in the world,

And you're also one of my best friends!

Dad,

You're such an incredible person,

I've never met anyone quite like you! You're unique!

If I could grow up to be even half the man you are,

That would be a blessing! I'm so proud to be your son,

And even prouder to call you my father!

Dad,

There's a song that reminds me of you:

It's called 'You raise me up', originally by Secret Garden.

The chorus goes: *"You raise me up, so I can stand on mountains;*

You raise me up, to walk on stormy seas;

I am strong, when I am on your shoulders;

You raise me up to more than I can be."

Dad, truer words were never sung.

This Is What Happens When

This is what happens when you realise the door is locked and your carer is outside:

When you first realise the door is locked,
The S-word springs to mind. After all, you're home alone, you don't know when your family's back, and you thought the door was unlocked, but you were wrong.
You panic for a second;
You're an anxious person, so why not!
Then, you notice what's locking the door;
A small metal part is vertical instead of horizontal.

You tell your carer to hang on, and that you'll fix it. You must fix it… you really need to pee! And you need a shower, so you really must find a way to unlock the door!
You drive over to the door, then realise you of course can't reach the metal part!
So, you turn your wheelchair around and try to reverse up to the door, before turning sideways to be horizontal with the door;
This takes a few attempts—
You're not a good driver,
(And you probably made marks on the wall again),
Even after so many years of driving your chair!

Eventually, once you are lined up horizontally with the door,
You try to push the metal part sideways—
Which is of course, not easy when your hand trembles
(Fine-motor skills have never been your strong suit with CP),
And the S-word springs to mind again as you try to
Push the part,

Push the part,
Push the part!

And then somehow,
In amongst all the pushing and sweating and hyperventilating,
Your mind wonders to turning this into a poem, just like you
did with "Highlighter". What a thought in a moment like this!
And then somehow,
You notice the part you've been pushing is now horizontal!
You back away from the door, press a button on the wall and
the door opens! Your carer, who's been patiently waiting
outside for the past ten minutes, enters. You wipe your brow,
grateful to be heading to the shower.
After all, you need a shower after this!

To Mack's Future Children

To Mack's future children:

You are, for now,
The one guarantee I have of becoming an uncle;
I do not know whether the rest of my blood or chosen families
will have children yet,
But I know he will. I just wanted to say hi.

At this point,
I should mention we are not brothers by blood;
This will no doubt explain why I have a British accent,
And your father has an American accent.
He's not only my best friend, but also my chosen brother,
And he chose me to be one of your uncles.

Let me tell you about your father:
He will give you an education in musical history;
Teach you classics like Elvis and Michael Jackson,
Icons way before your time,
But always worth listening to!
And your father is also a wonderful musician;
Might teach you a thing or two!

Your father is one of the best people I've ever known.
You'll always be loved by him,
He will love you 'til he bursts.
You'll always feel safe;
Nothing is taboo or out of bounds with him,
Nothing too irrational or crazy to be discussed,
He will never judge you. Especially not for your mistakes.
He will always help you see the light in the dark,

And better yet, he will be the light himself;
Be that beacon of hope for you,
As he's always been for me.

How do I know all of this?
You may ask.
I've known your father for a long time now;
And by the time you're in his life,
I hope to have known him for even longer.
Everything I've said about him couldn't be truer.
Trust me,
We've both needed each other over the years;
He will never let you down.

Your father's had his fair share of hardships;
Sometimes doubts himself,
As I doubt myself.
But in these moments,
It will be our job to remind him
How he makes our worlds a better place;
And that everything will turn out right.

You will have Skype calls with me,
As your father and I now have frequently.
We will tell you stories,
Most of which haven't happened to us yet,
And you'll probably hear the one about how we first met.

When your father adopts you,
He will change your life.
He may even save it.
I may tell you the story of how he saved mine,
But I'll save that one for another time.

I have no idea what kind of uncle I'll turn out to be;
In time we shall see.
But your father,
Your father will be the best father he can be;

I know he'll be magnificent.

Until then,
Love from your Uncle Eyar!
Your father and I,
Can't wait until
You're in our lives.

Priceless

I relish in the happiness of every single person I care about;
Their happiness is priceless.
Their happiness makes me happy;
No matter whether the subject is tickets to an Artic Monkey's
concert,
Or managing to repair a kayak!
No matter how big or small the event,
I relish in the happiness of every single person I care about.

My best friend recently celebrated his 1-year post top surgery
(In medical terms, this means 1-year post having a double
mastectomy),
And I think back to the year before:
When my father and I donated $50 towards the surgery.
My father didn't have to donate with me;
He did so because he appreciates the impact Mack has on my
life.

I think back to that donation;
My half felt, and still feels, grossly inadequate.
Anything I would've given him would feel inadequate;
There's nothing I could do to repay him for what he's done
for me;
Lifts this transman to a place where I feel all is, or will be
okay,
And my dreams are possible.
Has faith in me
Even when I doubt myself,
His friendship is priceless.
And the donation was one of many ways of lifting him the
way he lifts me.

I think back to the first Skype call after his surgery.
I asked if he was happy;
A question I already knew the answer to,
But to see his face bloom,
To see the joy in his grin,
The sparkle in his eyes,
That, that was worth every cent of the donation;
I'll never forget it!
It's hard to believe we were both suicidal, closeted transmen
when we first met.

My best friend recently celebrated his 1-year post top surgery.
Mack's now the happiest he's ever been;
A constant reminder that my medical transition is possible
too,
That this kind of peace is possible too,
That I can make these dreams come true,
Mack is alive.
And I, am alive.
We are both alive,
And I couldn't be happier for him!
'Cause to see him happy in his own skin,
That,
Is priceless!

String

"There is magic in long distance friendships",
I read in a quote.
Well, ain't that the truth!

I met him across the ocean;
We're over four thousand miles apart,
But he heard my satellite call,
And has been my best friend ever since.

His name is Mack.
Mack's the reason there's always a piece of me in America;
Despite having never been yet,
A piece of me will always be by his side.

His friendship is like gold dust;
It doesn't matter how long the distance string is;
Whether we move farther or closer in proximity,
Is irrelevant.

Because there is another string;
The string of our bond.
It is tied to him, and it is tied to me.
This string only gets stronger over time;
Pulling us closer in heart,
For every mile we're apart.
It doesn't care about geographical barriers;
Human connection surpasses every obstacle.
Despite the distance, Mack knows the real me
Better than most people.
I hope our bond never breaks.
My friend, Meggie, understands this, too;

Meggie also has internet friends in different countries.
And has the same relationship with some of them,
As I have with Mack.
Meggie's also friends with Mack;
The three of us have a whale of a time on Skype together!

Whenever Meggie and I meet Mack in person,
Or whenever Meggie meets their other internet friends,
It'll be magnificent every time.
But, until then,
We know that what we have
Can only be defined by us. Nothing else
Really matters.

Long distance friendships, and other forms of long distance
relationships,
Are proof that the string of connection is not easily broken;
No matter what we're faced with.
And isn't that,
Just magical?